THE GREAT PROMISE

GENESIS 12:1 – 21:3 FOR CHILDREN

Written by Alyce Bergey

Illustrated by Betty Wind

ARCH Books

CONCORDIA PUBLISHING HOUSE LTD., LONDON, E. C. 1
MANUFACTURED IN THE UNITED STATES OF AMERICA

ISBN 0-570-06034-6

Most people long ago forgot
what great things God had done.

They prayed to gods they made from gold–
or to the moon or sun!

Now Abraham, an old man, lived
among those people, too.
But God said,
"You must leave this place!
To stay here will not do."

"Where will I go?" cried Abraham.
"Lord, I don't understand."
The Lord said, "I shall show to you
a new and different land.
A nation's father you will be
and I shall bless you, too.
And EVERYBODY will someday
be blessed because of you!"

So Abraham took down the tents.
His servants helped him tie
upon the donkeys' backs their goods
and all of their supplies.

"Where are you going?" asked his friends
and neighbors in surprise.
"I do not know," he answered them.
Some cried, "This is not wise!"
And others laughed, "You're moving and
you don't know where you'll go?
Ridiculous! We've never heard
such foolishness, we know."

But Abraham said, “I must go,
for I have heard God’s call.”
Though people laughed, he helped his wife
up on a camel tall.

The caravan began to move –
each sheep and frisky lamb,
each donkey, goat, and wobbly calf.
"Good-bye!" said Abraham.

They started out across the plains,
the sandy hills, and rocks.
Some servants went ahead; they drove
their master's herds and flocks.

Old Abraham and Sarah jogged
along on camels' backs.
Behind them came more servants and
the donkeys with their packs.

At night the caravan would stop.
Beneath the stars they slept.
Some servants watched to see that no
wild beasts upon them crept.

Then on they trudged day afte
till they were tired and weak.
At last they came to Canaan la
They stopped. They heard God

"Now here's the land that I shall give
your children after you."
"We have no children!" Sarah cried.
Said Abraham, "That's true."

"But I believe God's word," he said.
"Come, let us celebrate!"
They built an altar to the Lord,
then feasted long and late.

"You please me, Abraham," said God.
"I'll give you a reward!"
"What will it be?" asked Abraham.

"A son!" declared the Lord.
"Someday, dear Abraham," said God,
"I promise there shall be
more people in your family
than all the stars you see!

"And I shall be their God; yes, they
will be My people, too."
"Oh, I believe Your promise, Lord!"
cried Abraham. "I do!"

Then Abraham put up their tents
beneath an oak tree high.
And in their home in Canaan land
year after year went by.

Soon Abraham was rich – his flocks
and herds all grew and grew.
He said one day, "God blessed us as
He promised He would do."

"Though God has blessed us," Sarah said,
"with things like flocks and gold,
He also promised us a son.
But now we are too old!"

Old Sarah wept, and Abraham
was puzzled: Could it be?
Was Sarah right? But one day as
he rested 'neath his tree,

he saw three men in front of him.
He bowed down at their feet.
He said, "Stop here and rest awhile.
I'll bring some food to eat."

The men agreed; so Abraham
ran to his herd and looked
until he found his finest calf
and brought it to be cooked.

He said to Sarah, "Bake some cakes."
And when a meal was made,
he took it to his guests outside.
They ate it in the shade.

One of the guests said, "Soon your wife shall have a baby boy."
"THIS IS THE LORD!" thought Abraham. His heart was filled with joy.

The Lord said, "You and Sarah now
are very old, it's true.
But there is not a THING that is
too hard for God to do."

The Lord then thanked them for the food
and with His angels went.
Old Abraham and Sarah waved
good-bye beside their tent.

They laughed with joy, for now they knew
that they would have a son.
Said Abraham, "This day has been
a very special one."

When springtime came, their son was born.
Yes, Isaac, he was named.
"Lord, nothing IS too hard for You!"
old Sarah then exclaimed.

Their friends all came to celebrate
the wonderful event.
The promised family now began
with this small boy God sent.

And Father Abraham became,
as his whole family grew,
King David's great-great-grandfather
and Christ, our Savior's, too!

DEAR PARENTS:

The story of Abraham is a story of a great faith and of a great promise. It is, above all, the story of a great promise, to which Abraham clung with his whole being and on which he was willing to stake his entire security.

God promised to aging Abraham something that meant everything to him: a family, one with a glorious destiny, a permanent tie to God, and a land to call its own. In God's promise to Abraham there was His wonderful plan for the salvation of all men, for the salvation we have in Christ was long in the making. It was being prepared in the entire history of the Hebrew people, beginning with Abraham. As the Gospel of Matthew (1:1) puts it, Jesus Christ was "the Son of David, the Son of Abraham."

Will you help your child see the excitement of God's promise to "Grandfather Abraham" and of Abraham's adventuring into the unknown at God's call? His clinging to God's promise when all odds seemed against it? And will you help him see how God's promise was fulfilled in the unfolding history of His people Israel, with its climax in the coming of Christ, the Messiah?

THE EDITOR